MW01702952

Storm still

Storm still

David O'Meara

HARBINGER POETRY SERIES
an imprint of
CARLETON UNIVERSITY PRESS

ISBN 0-88629-360-X (paperback)

Printed and bound in Canada

Canadian Cataloguing in Publication Data

O'Meara, David, 1968-
Storm still

(Harbinger poetry series ; 7)
ISBN 0-88629-360-X

I. Title. II. Series

PS8579.M359S86 1999 C811'.54 C99-900818-8
PR9199.3.O47S86 1999

Cover and author photos: Jeff Hardill
Design and interior: BCumming Designs

The epigraph on page 1 is from Percy Bysshe Shelley's "Julian and Maddalo," and that on page 35, from Albert Camus' "The Minotaur, or The Stop in Oran," in *The Myth of Sisyphus and Other Essays.*

Carleton University Press gratefully acknowledges the support extended to its publishing program by the Canada Council and the financial assistance of the Ontario Arts Council. The Press would also like to thank the Department of Canadian Heritage, Government of Canada, and the Government of Ontario through the Ministry of Culture, Tourism and Recreation, for their assistance.

Harbinger Poetry Series, Number 7

This book is for my parents,
William and Dorothy O'Meara
—with love and gratitude.

CONTENTS

STORM STILL

AXIS
MUNDI

Life is not a stroll across a field.
—a Russian proverb

I love all waste
And solitary places, where we taste
The pleasure of believing what we see
Is boundless, as we wish our souls to be:
And such was this wide ocean, and this shore ...
—Shelley

DEBUT

I broke the record for the hundred
yard dash at the tender age of nine;
across uneven pasture and pursued
by a bull. He was the hulking monster

of my preteen terror, and truth
was the moment when I broke the horizon
above the creek, chanting silently for
his absence. If lucky, only the cattle

appeared, fanning the sun with long lashes, lazy
and untroubled at their saltlick opium dens.
Only one hundred yards from creek to gate,
but you knew the bull was somewhere, sharpening

his tools, plotting your destruction.
I stumbled when I saw him coming, shot
for the six aged creaks of wooden slats
that announced each step to escape, caught

the top and swung free—all the while,
the tall grass stroked like violins.
Then the brute stuttered to a nonchalant
walk, eyeing me sideways like some snide

rival who'd stolen all the glory, little
kingpins or nature's mafioso. And there, for
a moment, we stared through the bars that split
the beast from boy, he watching my intact

skull that puffed in exhaustion out embarrassed
red cheeks, denied the romance of carving
out a message on the trunk
of my body. And I, who had

screwed up my face at even the mention of
flowery things, traced a delicate step home,
past waterbugs and the soft bullets
of cattails, holding my breath—

ON RURAL ROUTE #7

I remember the sharp whack of
a knife cutting through carrots
on the bare wood table—
                                        a real good whack,
that echoed across the kitchen
on R.R. #7
There, a stiff parliament of cupboards
lorded over the counter
that stretched past both sides
of a stove
              busy in its temperatures. At five,
a sizzle struck up, then
the tap and click of cutlery that
trickled to silence when cued
by the kettle's whistle.

                                A well-built house
leaves space to creak, the way strength
and weakness shape rhythm, and rhythm
rows into memory. How
ill-fitted glass chatters in wind-tapped frames,
and tiles that dip in an uneven floor
become keys of a massive accordion,
wheezing and breathing under
the pressure of familiar feet.

In that rhythm I played
into the strum of my pulse, began
the half-whispered apologies
for the heart and
mind that will never agree.
Too young to know, I had begun the slow
journey out of myself,

seeking to fall in step,
to curl into a sound and rage in
my own circumference
like the bond between
clapper and bell-cup.

On hurried half-dressed
mornings, trying to stanch the flow of minutes
as the school bus crested the hill;
with the screen door crash, in my mother's
worried goading,

in the work-day thump of my father's steeltoes.

Past midnight, I could tiptoe
across the basement carpet, blindly aware of when to
duck
my head around the pipe
and fit my hand
to each doorknob
like a private weathered glove.
High above, the attic sat like a ship's hull
in the off-season, moored
upside-down, deep and ribbed.
With its lights left on, it gazed across
the lawn to study the highway, till
someone would notice, climb
the twisted stair
and tug the bare bulb
out.

Awake so late, muffled voices ebbing
through bedroom vents, sleep still
hours away,
the clock, like a cat, scratching at the bedpost ...
Just the silence beyond,
and the beating of blood, the furnace's

Gregorian hum rising and dipping
through the unsettled timber of night—

VERANDA

The horizon's equilibrium: a corrugated
field holds up the blue shelf
of a perfect afternoon.
Here is October, still warm but coolly snapping
the clothesline's white sheets.
Fenceposts stiffen, the days run shorter;
colder.
Sparrows and blackbirds, like sweetness
and sorrow, raid the same feeder.

They skirt the idle ditches,
                                        salivary
and thick with the bulk of leaves
and soggy grass, cut and left to whither.
Before the kids are called to supper,
you can sit and
        hear the cars
as they step into gear,
and study the quick
scatter that's always happening between gravel
shoulder and forest, stirring up
the sheer blinding beauty
              of a pine-soaked road.

              A surface chill spreads
along the arms, warning that soon
the attic must be abandoned, the veranda
opened only for storage.
A boy in a red jacket passes, thick
gloves on, head lowered
so his lashes catch the sudden
release of rain,
so he won't be blinded by headlights.

It's days like this we wish for things

we know would be impossible.

A BACKYARD MAP

Football in the afternoon—
I'm hunkered at the scrimmage line
on the spot
where my sister got clipped
                    by a snowball
laced with a razor of ice.
She crumpled, bleeding crimson splashes
on the white skidoo track
until we pulled her home
shrieking through the drifts.

My cousin bled like that over
horseshoes and beer bottles
    when a missed ringer took him
    right in the shin.
Or a brother down on patio blocks,
knocked windless
against the picnic table, splinters
like buckshot
spiking his ribcage.

Tackled on the spruce-tree sideline,
I roll and retrace the landmarks
                    of each near-disaster,

                                        remember
the drunken slip on a backyard rink—the crunch
of tailbone—stomach queasy,
too frightened to move,
knowing,

just knowing
I'd landed funny.

Like that instant
with the right
foot
caught and chattering
through mower blades:
time drawn taut, traffic shooshing
somewhere beyond the mind's queer buzz,

all my half-baked notions
crammed into one pure sliver of clarity.

As the uncle that day
whose heart said *ta hell with it*,
then shuddered, took
a last gulp of autumn wind,
and crashed the rig of his body
into the woodpile.

I'm thinking of it now with
the sun in my eyes,

as I turn
to face the long bomb.

AXIS MUNDI

Mid-August and on the lawn
children are hopping the length
of a wooden ladder found lying
in a depth of uncut grass.

They stretch out their arms, one
foot is pointed and poised to geiger
for gravity's centre as they size
up the square between the slats

of each jump. Kicked, the rungs and
uprights stiffly squeak with rusted joints.
The children stare hard in tensed
concentration, all of them together

but each alone in their turn, smack-
dab in the balance of the acres. Nothing
to worry about, not the sun's burnished gloam
or the thick air cooling. For them

and at this time of day, as
light and sound quaver, sponged by
hay bales, the transit of evening slows
so twenty steps might feel like years

and the slippery longitudes of their passage
dangle a chill down every backbone.

AUGUST

All that will burn has gone
into the swaggering bonfire
to scorch the numb expressions of those
who lean too close, the beach-kiln
baking each retina,
          stares glazed in their sockets.
Above the zenith of flame, somewhere
midnight came and passed

like a spirit no one has witnessed
                    but all believe in,

and your friends, one last summer away
from high school diplomas
swig Molsons, toast
with gin mickeys and mason jars of rum.
Your two hands throb in firelight, recognized
but unreal, like arcane puppets you
found in a trunk and have learned to manipulate.
Music, voices, charred shavings of tinder
cartwheeling through smoke, emotions
like touch paper in the faces at the fire,
like smudges on acetate.

You blink at the heat-blast where black logs convulse.
In slow-mo, questions circle
outward from alcohol's inept sorcery.
A sleight of hand, a few more tips
of the bottle, and you tip
out of yourself.
And something sifts
through the stars as you conjure
for an image of who you might become,

one blink away before it disappears.
And that missed chance is August.

Beyond the dying glow
on trance-steady bodies—that coven
of friends, a fire-tinged fresco
of t-shirts and bra-straps—you stroll
to touch the damp sand where freshwater
laps at discarded shoes.
You toss your answers to the water, driftwood
time may smooth.
All that will burn has gone.
A nib-line of dawn scrawls across
night's last charcoal sketch,

and in that dark parchment something
is writing you—
your pencilled silhouette shivers but
will not move, waiting for a password or signal
that may never be sent
          and none could verify.

FIELD-CROSSING

The clover's razed; the ground is autumn-hard. The land
bristles in a ragged frame. I'm on the far end, watching

weightless clouds hastened

by wind, the day dark but huge with a muscled rustling.
A hydro-pole impales the midriff of the field—a world-tree

ripe with announcements; a pivot staking sight—imperious

and actual against the numbing pace of flat horizon.

First frost tonight. Silver power-lines stretch into the distance, on
and on, beyond the fenced concessions.

I still have not set out.

SOUNDINGS

TRANS-CANADA

Trying to describe it, you stand
at one end, thinking it's a drainpipe
where cars trickle and stop, catch
themselves on towns
                          and settle forever.
One day the road is a zipper
and as you drive
                               you zip and uncover
the hairy blonde chest of Saskatchewan.
On another, it's a gallery of glass and metal.

Traveling it, passing bent fences
sunk to the wire, shifting your weight
between each foot
while nightfall darkens a roadside of red-
veined granite,
                                         you'll believe anything
and imagine it to exhaustion—
the highway a warped seesaw
                          balanced on Superior,
St. John's and Victoria perched at each end.

If you go, start at night
so home is a porchlight that shivers
in memory, each spotlit roadsign
hung in a batter of black.
The far-off and further-on
            have yet to become unyielding,
the brain's grey fingers can still caress its empty thoughts
            until the map's sheer distance
drains away confidence
and you anxiously grip
the steering wheel—as if your hand could
clutch the engine like a baseball

and throw it at the ocean.
A lean odyssey of hours, a country
only skimmed, the highway's
a hairless cut on Ontario's lumberjack beard,
a place where trucks pass like thunderstorms,
highbeams like scattered lightning.

And bright days, the sun seems tired,
but burns with a typhoid
frenzy, consuming itself there
in the desert of the sky.

All this time, you've been driving
with a murderer's stare, rubbing
at eyes to loosen the belt of exhaustion,
feet frozen in the vent's
                    sagging slats, body aching,
stomach full of apples and bagels
but not a damn thing
          coming out the other end.
And parting a clutch of maples
that arm-wrestle the clouds, inching
through fields drab as porridge,
                                        you drive until
you've thought yourself into
a furious silence that aches in the mind,
each naked contradiction
shining in fixity, grieving
for a wholeness you'll never grasp
but only glimpse in fractions
that shimmer
          like trout scales in moonlight.

Thinking you can never return, but
walk the earth until it's done,
honed to gather one handful of logic
while complexity deepens.

SPAIN

—for Jeff Hardill and Amy Allan

On your walls
a sanctuary of kitsch: angels shaped in plaster
fighting for space

with black velvet bulls.
Also, a dozen or so Christs, heads bent down in sorrow
from each perfect

sacrifice. I think
of those countries where history's chiselled in icons,
a racket between

rifle and crucifix
that rattles down through the red red wounds
of the world.

Sooner or later
the bulls will eye the angels, they'll fix
their flowing tunics

in one red squint
of focus, and charge like an untended cylinder
breaking from the block.

And the angels
will take their stand, waving a scroll of pious
calligraphy.

We'll rise or fall
by our choice of which side to take
in order to count

among the survivors.
But the angel's just a figment dragging its shadow
through the vacuum

of heaven.
And the bull is slaughtered
on Earth.

SOUNDINGS

"History is not a random sequence of unrelated events. Everything affects, and is affected by everything else. This is never clear in the present. Only time can sort out events. It is then, in perspective, that patterns emerge." —William Manchester

"... the useless, the odd, the peculiar, the incongruous—are the signs of history." —Stephen Jay Gould

I SOUNDINGS

A fair while ago

I cracked the spine
of some thick book, lined with
tidemarks of science and history,

and into it, sent my plummet
down—a lead thought kissing
water—let it drop to bite

the surface-sheen and scurry
to the depths, dispensing itself
through a playful tug of undertow.

It tapped false shoals, snagged
weeds, jarred against the spar
of a sunken wreck below,

the sounding's length continually
unreeling where I'd come to take
one tributary's measure

and add that number to what
I thought I knew. And saw and guessed.
It's been years now, and still

that thread is paying out.
It has not touched bottom.
I begin to doubt

it ever will.

i) Provisions (Monday, September 19, 1519)

And how could we have known ...
Three-masted, rigged full-square, tall
and broad of beam—five
multi-decked galleons in all.

A store of rice, beans, cereal, cheese;
raisins, flour, garlic, peas

With three tons of pickled pork,
harpoons,

fishhooks;

seven-hundred pipes and butts of wine.
Helmets, lances, spikes, shields. Lines

of hawser.
Oakum, beeswax,
pitch and tar. Stacks
of lumber,
a weight of anchors—

With an hourglass, compass, and astrolabe.
With a black bushy beard and a penetrating eye.
With a calibrated guess and a few loose reports.

In the gulf between faith and reason,

how could we have known?

ii) Theories of the Earth (Departure)

A sixth-century monk
wrote the world was flat, though he'd been out-thought
for eight-hundred years, since the shadow cast
in one eclipse

displayed a sphere
to Aristotle. (The philosopher's case alleged
that land contains more weight than water,
so beyond the Hesperides, India
must be near

for the world to balance ...)
We kept this in account, though Columbus swore
he'd reached it; but not very much later
than that, Vespucci

confirmed the chance
it was another place altogether—a blemish on *Imago Mundi.*
Some gossip on a southern passage was what we had,
on terms to claim all land for profit
and glut our stores

with cinnamon, pepper,
nutmeg and cloves. For them it was a matter of business.
But you'd no picture of what you wanted, which made
you want it more.

That morning I won't ever
forget. From sleep I stirred and watched the window
go from black to emerald to a sinless blue,
the rooftops and harbour in glittering tow,
a perfect mirror

to the sun's steady course.
I gathered my sack and started down,
the last time standing
on such solid ground.

iii) An Unsuccessful Mutiny—Quesada's View (April 2, 1520)

"At San Julien he turned
his back
forever from the way we'd passed,

cutting the umbilical of our wake.

Patagonia's coast was the serrated blade
we dragged our prows beside, every
wide estuary a fake ghost hope
that thrashed in his cobalt stare.
A thousand miles ago, his voice had the tone
of a man with a long tale to tell. Now,
his mutterings drone.

Remember?
We tasted pineapple for the very first time.
                                        I soured—

but saw amused pleasure twist
behind his sticky mustache.
                    But those lips stayed
shut on our objective. No smile turned up
with each reported cove
                  and shallow sounding.
We'd sighted land a dozen times—
he was praying for an absence.

At latitudes further south, sleet
on the sails like a slab of silt, hail
rattled the nervous crew ...
Sea-grey, limb-frozen, worn out,

we argued retreat, our thin
veil of patience torn through—

With scant provisions, and
orders to tack on a steady course south,

we reached our own limit. I
stirred thirty men
to another ship, boarded
and knifed one loyal officer
six times
which severed any other complaint.
But in twenty-four hours
            he'd turned the tide,
the only mark his plans had ever changed
was me in the brig
awaiting trial, the outcome hardly
a troubled surmise.

Now we're on opposite
ends of the pole, but my torso pinned here
rots and drips to where
he surveys the deck below,

or looking up, seems uneasy.

A flaw in his own trajectory,
the glint in my eyes a maggot feast
pecked by alien birds.
From this vantage, a first glimpse
of that slippery passage.
If I could see ...

A kind of irony, at least—"

iv) Pacific (the outset—December 2, 1520)

No one should love this world,
but joy is simple. Not a cloud
to clutter the sky, the sea an uncut
jewel tumbling with light.

A plump canvass stuns the eye. Tired
but cool, the steady prow
is reaping like a scythe. The sun
is an open spigot. Our bodies are strong.

God help me, no one should love this world.

v) March 5, 1521

I had cornered a rat
as it made the upper deck, skittered and sat
at the foot of the jib—a meal within reach
I meant for myself—though at last count
they were worth half a ducat each.

No one was selling now—when
we'd pitched what remained of nineteen men
(their swallowing stopped with mouth-sores and swells)
into the drink and watched
numbly from the rails

as they floated away—stomachs distended
and flatulent, as if they weren't really dead,
just taking a swim. I was young, of nobility,
Venetian by birth, but had never forecast
this image of me:

frail, deranged, a raw effusion
of open sores. A walking vivisection.
As I tensed to lance the stricken rodent—something
left unnoted in my log—
a shatter of lightning

washed the air in white,
the moon's negation hanging like
a death's head at the feast. Our three galleons
were needles in the ocean's black sashes,
stalled at the hem of that constant horizon.

Three winter months and twelve-thousand miles were
then suspended in my eyes, sure
the light I saw was a match sparked up to show
me hell. This place was a well where we'd come to drown.
I knew that now.

Where you and I believed we were
was half-boast, half-blur.
A shade of current, a smell, the dampened cries
of birds. A stripe of dark enlarging ...
Landfall comes as a slow surprise.

vi) Death of Magellan (April 27, 1521)

Headstrong, exultant, drunk
on God; above, beyond, but sunk

in a swirl of pomp
and conversions, risen from

ashes of this scuttled disaster.
Reckless, bloated with rapture,

translucent with faith, gleaming
with buckles and blades, fever unfurling ...

Knee-deep in tide, smacked by stones,
sword-arm slashed, the white of bone

showing; helmet knocked clear and
speared in the cheek, Ferdinand

Magellan—Commander emissary
of his Christian majesty

of Spain—has mortally come to ground.
That slow journey around

and this cheap urgency. Magellan,
struck and spent like a coin from heaven.

vii)

Master, I heard traces of you list
and moan with the struggling timbers of
that rotten wreck, as our vessel gripped

the sight of home.

Of those
two-hundred and sixty-five
who manned five ships three years ago,

a crew of eighteen have weighed one anchor
in Sanlucar.

Master—
for a span of months I was drunk on wine
and spent such nights
          in the thighs of whores,
their eyes wide with wonder
with where I'd been, pleading for
descriptions of Gog and Magog,
griffins and dog-headed men.
          When a barman ripped up
my bill if I'd give an account
where the shores
of El Dorado lay, I told a more fantastic tale:

the truth.

The sea it took three months to cross,
and how we returned to this
very spot on waves
we never once retraced.
Then I looked him squarely in the face, and poured

this riddle in his ear:

    when we landed in Santiago, the year
    was 1522—Wednesday, the 9th of July
           as both logs showed.
    But in Santiago, it was Thursday,
                    the 10th.

The barman blinked—brows
crumpled like a bull—and
just to show me what he meant
I was tossed through
the window
       like a picador who'd
taunted with one too many blows.
I lay there by a broken cart, elbows
in horse-piss and rotting vegetables. An unbroken
line of stars dripped above
the pressing rooftops.
            Master,
no trace of you remains
from the battle in Mactan's surf.

The truth has a limit of days.

The planet moves
beneath my feet, the centres
are slipping from their guides.
Another axis turns the earth.

And how could we have known?

III TURTLE SOUP

i)

A pot of cut flesh,
a mix of carrots and celery.
An onion studded with cloves.

A bouquet garnish, some
salt, and pepper—dropped
in a clear, brown gravy,

boiled to a bubble. Gently,
a two-hour simmer.
Strained. Thickened. Diluted.

An aromatic infusion
of basil, chervil, savory,
and fennel—Mr. Charles Darwin,

present naturalist aboard
the H.M.S. *Beagle* is dipping
his spoon in the ship's rare pot

of turtle soup. Six p.m.
An unorthodox late supper.
He pockets a handful

of dried apples, steadies
his bowl in the palm
of his hand, zigs and

yawls through the midshipman's
berth to plunk himself
down with the captain

in his cabin. A bit of soup
splashed over the side,
speckled on the tabletop.

"How does the captain find it?"
Darwin inquires. FitzRoy raises
his rigorous stare, and finds it "tolerable."

Clearly, something is on his mind.
A lamp like a pendulum
above their heads, swinging

shadows across mahogany.
The puny cabin crammed
at every useful inch.

Darwin's carpet-bag on FitzRoy's
sofa. Microscope, compass,
magnifying glass,

a brace of pistols,
binoculars, shirts and uniforms.
Darwin's geological hammer.

(The crew have coined his nickname:
Our flycatcher.) On the floor,
jars of spirits for preserving bugs.

And in beds of sawdust,
twenty-two chronometers
tick and attest to FitzRoy's

fixation with exactness.
He leans back in his chair,
takes a sip of lemon juice—his

mustache like a worm across
his upper lip. The worm wriggles:
"I've been reading, at your

suggestion," the captain begins,
"entries from your journal. In
particular, those pertaining

to the islands of Galapagos."
On the table, beside
his shipmate's elbow, an archipelago

of open books. Darwin's
journal, FitzRoy's Bible,
Lyell's *Principles of Geology.*

The captain's finger is tapping
the flycatcher's scribbled notes.
FitzRoy quotes: *Here, both in space*

and time, we seem to be
brought somewhat near
to that great fact—that

mystery of mysteries—the first
appearance of new beings
on this earth.

The finger lifts and drops
to rest against his beak-sharp
nose—one that has

possibly caught the whiff
of theological mutiny.
Darwin takes a slurp of soup,

then maroons his spoon
on a side of the bowl.
The captain is sunk

in an eddy of gloom.
The Bible, well-thumbed,
is cracked wide at Genesis—

the testament to creation
as one instant of time.
What FitzRoy's finger has been

indirectly pointing at. Now
Darwin, pacing the room, careful
not to step on anyone's toes,

goes over all his mental notes,
arranging an explanation. A variety
of species in the same

island-group. All adapted
to suit diverse environments.
"Take these finches for example,"

(a linchpin, Darwin considers):
"their beaks, if you notice, differ
on every island, adjusted

to each available food." Thick
beaks for cracking nuts, others
smaller for snatching insects.

"You see? Isolation seems to favour
the origin of something completely new ..."
The captain is morose. Severely silent.

Darwin takes it down a peg.
"Of course, they're only jottings.
A jumbled attempt to come

to grips with a certain mystery.
Mere speculation." He takes a cue
from Lyell. "Like geologic

change, there seems to be
a process here. Development
of form and function

across both space and —"
A flurry of motion, an accidental slosh
that blurs the page of scripture.

Darwin has knocked his bowl
of red-hot soup across the captain's Bible,
drowning the print *And every thing*

that creepeth upon the earth.
The flycatcher sputters apologies
while sopping up the mess.

ii)

The captain up on deck,
commanding a sullen mood.
Space and time, he grumbles

under breath, then double-checks
the last of calculations on
a chronological reckoning.

Four years of measurements,
an accurate fix of longitude—
He can properly chart a six-week sail

till the cheerful sight of home.
No subtle shades of meaning there—
He knows precisely where he stands.

Darwin in the cabin, seasick—
worried the opposing temperaments
kept in careful distance

are slowly about to intercept.
He clambers through a hatchway, in
a move to smooth all doubts,

spies the captain digesting the stars.
Darwin spills his guts. Vomit
on the poop deck. Then, a deluge

of laughter erupts, captain and crew.
A balance restored again. Or broken.
Each world shattered as it forms.

IV ASCENSION ISLAND

A pace of latitudes
they pilot through, fathoms they dangle
over, tides they scuttle across

like a spider over sand.
Tossed like a trinket in storms, spun,
thrown off-course, but set

to ride each gushing wave, flat-on
to their ingrained goal.
Slung in that orbit, astride a private

border of the known, where
the horizon waits, glimmering
on the surf's surging turn;

through the groan, the creak of hemisphere's
hinge, the low choir of tidal murmurs
learning their pitch and tone practiced

when continents stuck and clung
like burdock in bloom—the turtles
swim for home—Ascension

shuddered in blood, pulled by the drone
of water slapping shore, steered
by a current's taste or smell,

the island's warming wake,
instinct's urge as lash and rudder.
Turtle—whitecap's companion, squat

disk of scutes and limb, hitcher
of drifts—honing
on the blip of island,

that dark pavilion of stone
spit from the mid-Atlantic ridge,
that dead-centre nub,

left-behind burr to tug and tear
the ocean's drifting sheet
shimmied from the old world's curve.

Turtle, through wrack, oiled ooze, two
thousand miles, no word or vessel
to capsize on unmarked coral,

no god in that green skull—
in the sweep and play, in silence,
no prayer but litany

just the same, that tells
the journey has carried on,
without the saying—

THE DESERT

"There is something implacable about the desert ... everything contributes to creating this dense and impassable universe in which the heart and mind are never distracted from themselves, nor from their sole object, which is man. I am speaking here of difficult places of retreat."

—Albert Camus

RAIN

—for Edward Thomas

I listen to the rain, a monotone
of trickles, taps, and spatters on stone.
Its sing-song cadence is unsteady;
the anthem to an empty mood. I envy
the sound, expected only to stammer
broken sea-chanteys like a weepy drinker,
as some days I am desperate to be
nameless, unhuman and beautiful. Many
dark days of rain you praised, Edward—

you sang the wet earth you were drawn toward
until it drank you down in Flanders.
The names, the studied sounds, the prayers
you scribbled out hang in the weather now,
as the glow of a streetlight makes shadows bow
where pine trees jig in the thunderstorm,
as if the ghosts of what you felt had form.

THE WAR AGAINST TELEVISION

I know about the time, as a child, you'd stare
beyond far-off cottages on the opposite lakeside
wondering how it would feel to die. Remember?
Do you? You were hardly serious then. We've all gone
through that stage, the bright half-terrible change
when first scanning stars, trying to grasp where distance

ends, but after a summer of thinking, that distance
carries on beyond comprehension, resistant to any stare.
To be young is a kind of trance that doesn't change.
Majesty, like terror, slips in from the side
like a wind, whose broad fluctuations seem gone
though that first stinging draught we remember.

Our thoughts make noise; we are what we remember,
are the love we've lived, are the traveled distance
our own stride made. All that seems gone
is every distracted hour spent with a vacant stare,
blankly accepting that nothing will form inside
of us, content that nothing should change.

Each year should be a gathering, not the exchange
only, of anticipation to regret. I remember
at sixteen, working gas pumps—summer job on the side
of Highway 62—I watched clouds advance in the distance
across a blackening hayfield. Pausing, I stretched to stare
at the downpour coming on, daylight gone

to a grim contusion; the heat, traffic, for a moment, gone.
A stark, clear, sheet beat straight down and didn't change
direction, the wet edge of it inching onward, luring my stare.
I saw the line of rain blacken asphalt, as I remember
the squall dashing through me, then spinning into the distance
west and beyond. A long while I stood beside

that dark highway. I wanted to stay right there, outside
myself looking in, attentive to every instant I had gone
through, reliving the days with a kept distance
even as I wanted to flee, hide, attempt to change
everything I had happened to be. The doubt I remember
still disturbs, like a mote that burns the pacified stare.

Living's impossible; a full-time job trying to change
ourselves into something we love before we're gone.
We can't catch our breath. No wonder we stare.

LITTLE BOYS

They rattle the alleys with rusted bikes, break
bottles and scatter. Seen to torment a dog
on its leash, they're only out until the curfew's abused,
until parental voices treble from the front doorstep.
Caught beating tin on the next-door
shed, they stand stock-still clenching

the tortured stick, hard-pressed to raise an alibi.

No colouring books, no connect-the-dots. They just
stay inside to gulp chips and pop, watching
a litany of sitcoms and video. You look in their
room, there's nothing to clean. Empty their
pockets—a shopper's ad and some cold hard cash.

If frustrated, they'll make a tight little
fist, but the baby fat shows. When at last they test
the stripped impulse to commit some
brutal act, there's no family cited on newscasts.
It's proof they're not human, never were:

Notice the way they take three steps at a time
up the stairs to bed, the way
they shy from the simplest of questions.
Raised without the need to form an inner fiction
they'll admit to nothing but murder.

DESERT SONNETS

I Dante

—for Jason Babstock

Ottawa was Hell or Purgatory
the night you arrived. You were chased by beasts
that couldn't be pinned, while I just clung by
human Reason; but was not in the least
aware of what tack to take, trying to
circumvent a wide limbo of my own.
We ghosted a journey, though we had no
point to come to, and circled up and down
the market streets, sharing a confusion
of who held the lead and who lagged behind.
We've had no method but a holding on,
and past this turning there's another kind
of waste to cross, our only direction
to compare some facts with other fiction.

II Lear

Split-open sky. Wind. Hammered heath. *Storm still.*
Icy rain is spiking the surface down.
In this place, the skyline can stretch until
its elbows crack, till each distraction drown.
All's leveled. No court or stiff procession
will suit my mood, just a troublesome bunch
of dim-wits whose one hopeless solution
is to crawl into a hovel and hunch
there till the thunder's gone. I'll not go in;
I'm past that now. I botched it up. And though
I've crossed this blasted space and learned how thin
the split is between true speech and fool's dumb-show,
rapture or earthly horror, I've had it.
Storm still. It's the knowing makes it tragic.

III Igjugarjuk

"When I was young, strange visions came and spoke
to me in dreams I could not interpret.
Disturbed, my parents sent for Peqanaoq,
who recognized the crisis, took and set
me on a sledge just large enough to hold
me, and pulled it out into the flat, vast,
and frozen Arctic night. There, I was told
to sit for thirty days, to wait and fast;
and thinking only of the Great Spirit
I was left to face that cold and brutal
month. My heart went numb, seclusion broke it
bit by bit. *Sometimes I died a little.*
Near the end, a spirit came. More or less,
I've learned what I know from that loneliness."

IV *The Voyage Out* (Woolf)

The years come on, then disappear. Lovers,
friends—each new loss echoes with the distance.
It seems you've just sat down and the movers
are taking the chairs again. That substance—
it's never really there; you feel motion
and try to measure how far you've traveled,
but there are no landmarks on an ocean.
There's only the mind—shell-shocked, unraveled—
homesick as you stare from your own front door.
Each departure holds a promise you can't
sustain. Like a round flat stone pitched from shore
and skipping off, the hope for what you want
will ebb. Waves flow where even light can drown.
A stone in your pocket, you'll follow it down.

V *The Old Man and the Sea*

To be born is to enter heroics.
To put to sea with some bait, in the flap
and catch of wind-cracked sails, and dare to fix
a course beyond the reach of snare or trap,
beyond secret treacheries and landfall.
To go there, to throw off your lines and wait.
It's the waiting that's the hardest of all—
sweatbeads tracking the sun's descent, irate
and glistening off the head's angry swell.
Be ready to shift with the pull, and not
leave slack too loose. Keep your course. Hold it well.
To be born is to sail a wreck that's caught
between two shores, and try to keep it pure.
Watch the breeze. *Take it as it comes.* Endure.

VI Postcard from Camus

I will be perfectly honest with you:
the heat's just awful. I wander half-dazed
through town, stopping to shake sand from my shoe
while cypresses shimmer in the heat-haze.
At night there's nothing to do except sip
gin and smoke cigarettes with the door shut.
It's too dangerous otherwise—a nip
to the store, that's all. I think I'll go nuts
if something doesn't happen soon. It's hell.
From dawn till dark we're fixed like specimens
under the sun's searing lamp; I can't tell
up or down, right from left, trapped in its lens.
I only love the brown bodies—young, alert,
and full of joy. Wish you were here.—Albert

MARQUEZ

He must have come from a place

with valleys grooved like records,
where stately music might play
when a hoe scratched the soil.
Where good weather held the town
like the news of a general
strike,
and lanterns
splashed shadows

darker than any light bulb.

Red dust blew. In the square, cats rusted. Generations
weren't cut by clear
progressions;
the months collected, and coffee
taxied insomnia through cool parlours

replete with roses and shrouds.

On every tool, there was a history of notches.
At each table, a place kept for the dead.

The work was back-breaking, but
clean and precise—
Love could not be analyzed, and blood
was a spill
from the heaped iron skillet
of an angry word.

The rivers flapped in sudden storms. Insects flushed.

And in the interminable swelter of

heat,
forgiveness bloomed
in a circadian rhythm, urged on
with cool downpours of laughter

that spread like a plague

in a mysterious country—

UM

—a pause word in English that some people
use more than 1,000 times an hour

The pause between
the heart's morse-beats,

a beat itself, or shadow, the ghost
of a long-dead phrase;
a throw-away note, a stall to reflect,
an intersection of speech and rest;
the lull that waits
on the tip of the tongue, a seed-word
to hum in meditation.

A promise, an evasion, a latent
soliloquy—a word without
tense, claim or stress. A nerve we track
through stuttered debate, a star
in the black
or the space in between.

A rumour of insufficiency.
A restless undertone ...

A precious syllable, a tongue-tied knot,
a metronome that ticks our talk;
a telegram tap, a faint articulation,
a testament to uncertainty, a gap

or hesitation.

Um. That's
what's left, a sound—both vague and brief.
A monument or offering to things unsaid,

the least expression of joy or grief.

Storm still

THIS PHOTOGRAPH

So here I am, dressed to kill—
leopard-skin shoes, expressionist
tie, with that
cat-swallowing-canary smile.
And there you are, to the nines, hair
flipped and flowery skirt, half-smashed
on wine, lashes
batted and shit-eating grin—Just
get a load of us.

Up here on the balcony, oblivious
to the street below, a pose without
apology, struck
between the rail and broken windows.

Take this photograph
like a polished stone, some glossy shell
snatched from a stretched-out span of beach;
treat it as a memory, a bone tossed
to a hungry dog, a keepsake to keep

or leave behind.
You don't need to carry it, as I
have done, from autumn
to autumn, slipped
in the sheets of various books,

tucked in a backpack
   from truckstop to terminal. After all,
it's not the object itself, but
the spirit of the thing—the traveler's art
of going light,
               but knowing
exactly what to bring.

VANCOUVER NOVEMBER

Soaked leaves clump in a sludge, pasted
to every crack and concrete walk.
East 10th streams away in a smeared
parade of soggy spruce and basted

stucco; porches with drenched timber
sag from the burden of countless, wet winters.
We have left all talking behind,
stiffen at words in this cage of rain,

morosely pace the halls, open doors
to watch the tomb-grey drizzle
of Sunday afternoon.
Our hearts are closed shallow drawers

left with some odds and ends.
Stagnant, chilled to the bone,
dampened by tomorrow's
nine-to-five, we hold those

hours against our years, like a curling
conch's tunnel, and hear
the hollow echo of ourselves.
Terrible November

what can we do with you?
In dripping jacket-sleeves, by
forced march, past economy cars
parked like children in their pews,

we slog eight blocks with
granite expression for rye and a few
dark pints, feast and brood
on brass and varnished wood, the arith-

metic of rain ticking against
the sill like beads on an abacus.
Whatever counts the months, counts us
here, our feet so unsteady.

We must learn to risk that slip off-
centre—and make amends
for this shifting ground—the balance
that carries us to day's end. And street-ends ...

A HALF-REMEMBERED YEAR

Honestly, I don't know who ran
the machines this summer. The year began

stillborn in a frozen deadlock—
spring never came, we just rocked

and shuffled in the cold, storefronts still
frosted two weeks into April, until

over four sudden days, the city
simmered in every shadow, humidity

gearing up into a muggy damp.
We sweated and sweated, climbed the ramp

of summer's warehouse, and gathered the dry
stacks of our anger and sorrow inside

us. I don't know if I talked
to anyone. I can't imagine what

I could've said. But when the sun's doors
would open and dry off all the coarse

gobs of dew, I raced to every
street corner, endlessly expecting to see

you when I stopped. I never did.
You'd already packed and slid

away to another continent, fair warning
and all. I'd been half-crazy trying

to track these tremors that bled
the voice of reason from my head

and gripped this life like I was
a stick to be pointed, but always

at you. It seems so simple: speak what
you feel, and everything else, just keep your trap shut.

But none of that meant anything to me.
Your smile was a shot of rye whisky,

and when you'd pour out that bucket of brown
dusty hair, I'd choke and feel about to drown.

I'll shape my heart, now that you've gone,
to fit the sleeping echo of your bones.

FLOORBOARDS
—for Dorothy Jeffreys

It was worse than we expected, they told
us the next morning, wide-eyed and tight-lipped
at the faulty wiring tucked away for years.
From London, we arrived at the house in

darkness; it was past eleven, the two
of us tired and anxious to roam the south
of Wales. The floor inside had been torn up,
the electrical wire's tested age now

relented. Fighting the front lock, we cursed
at the calamity (one day early and
in another continent) and almost
lost our legs stumbling through the fuddle that

crouched in cross-beams under the carpet's popped
parasols. The workmen returned the next
morning, thinking they'd tidy things up to
buffer the blow.
We met them at the door.

Ha—you should have seen their faces. Like shocked
raccoons caught in the bin, the floorboards pulled
and piled against the walls, beds stacked tight with
storaged junk like tired seals mobbed on the beach.

They were forced to replace each switch and plug
in the house, and excise varicose wire.
Then said *it be a fortnight*. That's ... two weeks.
Only one stove element worked, hot baths

became long pot-and-kettle procedures.
Stripped, the stairs were canal locks in repose.
Two weeks of knocks and nails, the clutter of
drill bits: the whole house seemed to be winking
at us.

We couldn't complain. How could we?
We were foreigners fumbling with latchkeys,
Groucho Marxing through the dark but trying
to keep our slapstick to a minimum.

Denied luxury, we watched the weather
sip the minutes of each hour, then swallow
whole days in a gulp. We read in daylight,
forced to flex the different muscles of

time and location. Supper was an hour
before darkness stole the cupboards, dusk fell
and ushered us to candles, while morning
came on one side and left on the other.

FEBRUARY DIVORCE

Like a stashed-away witness I pace
the rooms, afraid to speak, worried
my words will tally the votes against me.
But I don't go anywhere. I just shift
and settle, a seafloor imitation.

February's clamp is tightening. To step
outside's to curse in this Canadian cold;
fingers turn to twigs in a block's walk, they'll
snap right off if you bend them.
And watching the skyline's slow divorce

from the light at dusk is not so glorious
when watched and watched. What's gone
is the surprise of seeing, the artless
gleam of horizon stolen in the moment.
The hours rub, pinched and deadened.

A penitent Horatio, I'd been chasing
a hair in the tub for two hours,
then slipped and dropped the towel in.
Past plans are pulled shingles
in need of repair. With each gesture

I have grown unsteady and obvious, as if
my legs finished off with pencil points.
It's funny what the mind goes through, how
the body just walks and walks. How the heart
seems lost, angry with everything—then resigns

to count the days, trading them away—

It's so funny.

DECEMBER, 6 A.M.

Full-grey, first light floats
inside this airy hour like smoke inside
a bottle. One bird
addresses the mountains, though
the mountains refuse to answer,
brooding from the broken parapet of themselves.
Each day, like newspaper, the sky prints
the same blurry snapshot of the sea,
which the wind then delivers.
And the sun—?
                    The sun
can't be found, though they
talk of it constantly, the bird, sky
and wind,
while I let the kettle
burn dry,

and hustle for dreams under eiderdown.

CHINESE QUINCE

Too heavy to rustle, the waxy
leaves of this Chinese quince
are a wardrobe of stagy green, dressing
the terrace-end of my year-long residence.

A juice blooms through the fruit, uncertainly
bitter. Taste tangled in its cells
strangles the stem with weight. Late,
late November, these reluctant perennials

cling and delay the seasonal guillotine,
swaying like lanterns that gutter and flare.
I watch them silently ripen, strain under
seams of pulp, simmer with a sun-yellow glare

and shake in the frost-edged glances
of wind. My landlady will come soon,
with a stick to strike them down.
Autumn will end in one afternoon.

FRICTION

The month stiffens with autumn's first bluff.

The chilled carafe of winter is tipping,

and I can taste a scene from Montreal, now
5 years past, a blind blast
of snow squeezing narrow streets
                                        in folded loads of white.

That was the year our plans fell through.
Circumstance set us arguing.
                                                                          Against
each other, against ourselves, around
each dusky blunder committed in the criminal
dark of January;
committed to our unswervable lease.
                                                              Snowbound,
we fought like two soldiers in Siberian retreat—
Complaints and caresses with all that time, we made
our bodies and our minds hard and sharp
and rubbed them together
                                                    to make a fire.

Worry, rapture, anger, age—
the same friction that stirs such energy
is wearing us away.

Tonight, sparse flurries spindle down,
frail as worn fabric, cold like a cage.
My body argues for the counterweight
of yours.
                                        Rubbed flesh excites flesh,
the quiver of nerves we touch and release, breath-
short and hurried, fearing fragility
or wanting it.

LAMINAR FLOW

It went off without a hitch; north-west, County
Rd. 28 to Algonquin Park in an early
October bid to circumvent Thanksgiving.

Jeff behind the wheel, the borrowed car gliding
like a bobsled toward Grand Lake, the red
and yellow-spackled forest undressing as we drove . . .

we outran the blackened clouds to a campsite,
slapped the tent into shape (two pegs missing from
the set), and tied a tarp above—stretched

and knotted to four stout birch—while squirrels
chattered in branches overhead, insanely jealous
of our opposable thumbs. Dinner in the halo

of an open fire; franks, beans, and Valpolicello
crackled in our stomachs. Though it poured all night
we were dry as dust. Our sleep was hard and curt

as a bullet. (The only snag was the shivering
piss at 4 a.m., when we watched the ghostly
prying beam of a train 20 clicks away, worried

it was actually a UFO, for fear we'd be obliged
to tell someone.) Hot chocolate and porridge, a
shuffle at dawn along the misty shore, we saw more

rainclouds protesting our stay with dark signs
beyond the woods. No worries. We packed up
like a M.A.S.H. unit and were smoothly

gone by afternoon. Pride goeth before the fall.
The car bouncing like a ball past the park exit,
a squirrel squirted from the underbrush,

a souvenir that stiffened in the rearview mirror.

IKIME-JINJA

"As soon as we become motionless, we are elsewhere ..."
—Gaston Bachelard

I ARRIVAL

The first hour after the airport,
my arm snug around you in
the taxi—my widened, utterly
unsettled eyes struggled between
the ongoing shock of three sights:

that street lit by headlights, the cabbie's
white gloves, and the precious thrill
of your grin framed in the backseat window.
What was going faster, I couldn't tell—
the car's chaotic lunge

or our fervent words tripping with talk ...
I checked the light beyond
the dash. Shops hurled by, red lanterns
and the colour-crazed blaze of pachinko
parlours—the only signs I could understand.

The cab dipped, lurched, and began to leave
the city behind as we climbed the twisting hill—
and I felt strange on the Earth,
and pictured it as an astronaut
would: shadowed and tragic

in a resin of blackness, a frail beacon
signalling in the starlit abyss. The cab door closed;
we'd paid the fare. I was standing there
somewhere among the months
and nothing recognizable.

II PLANETARIUM

Numerous nameless streets I'd have to
get used to; a local maze built
to suit the river's bend toward the ocean, with
walled-in concrete hillsides, the tight file of
housing and perfect backyard shrubbery—
It was all flawlessly foreign to me.

Street lamps were rare.
After sunset, a row of curtained windows
were limited guides to the right
way back.
                That time we went to a lecture
on stars, watched the false projected sky
across a planetarium dome, and thought
I might guess my way home
by picking

and linking what hung overhead,
but found I remembered nothing
                without a fat red arrow
and translated audio tape.

The only constellation I ever learned
was the route we tracked there, shaped by the points
of grocery store, library and shrine,
coffee-shop,

and our clanging aluminum door.

III RICE FIELDS

Down in the rice fields, the frogs
are fornicating.
It's spring after all.

Orgasmic croaks scherzo
and ride the heavy air,
the paddy squares teeming

and clamorous, a steady
froth of sound
that carries through the murk.

We wade into the orgy, giggling
and awed. The whole
glum brood is at it,

groaning for release, and we exchange
glances, gleaming and
pleased by this stew

of green voices churning through the gloom.
Up the road, carlights round
a corner, surprise our

silhouettes, and carve us statued
and listening on night's
backdrop. The chorus

clicks and stutters. Sound
shuts. Our whispers like stones
crashing down an incline.

IV FESTIVAL AT IKIME-JINJA

Two backroads reached there; two
paths up opposite sides that joined
at steps on a rustic plateau, forested
and lined with stone lanterns, where

this evening, the way is flamed
with red booths, like bonfires strung along
the curling rise to the *torii* gate—
not quite pilgrimage, but county fair.

Vendors offer octopus or squid, fried
corn, french fries or black seaweed
piled in papery tomes, while farmers
sharpen sickles near Disney shirts

and software. This hour's scene
both calms and makes us sick
for home. The familiar green of
cedar or pine—or the clean line

of a Japanese angle, shadow-praising
and spare—surface suggesting depth—as if
each place holds a hint of other landscapes
somewhere in the dark extent

of its own topography—

V DEPARTURE (ALBA)

We woke to the alarm, early—but stayed
under blankets as long as we could, not wanting to face
the cold floor, the coffee, the last-minute
reminders that led

to a third-floor descent and slow busride
into the airport's unnatural breeze.
We held that clasp until there wasn't a choice,
then pulled our bodies

out from the snug nautilus of the bed. Three months—so
little, so much, and it's already time.... As we turned
toward town, I pointed to all the shortcuts
I had started to learn.

A row of trees fenced the boulevard, the day
bright with blossoms that were just beginning
to show. Dorothy, I don't want to stay
and I don't want to go.

VANISHING POINT

Pedaling into noon through
grey intersections ...

after a confusion of warehouses
and boxed yards
with half-hidden sidestreets where
cars like weasels
would squeal and stab,

there was a slow slope up

on a ridge that ran flat

to an opening

and the ocean spread out its blanket.

The spokes whisked brightly in the air's
salty lick
and I circled the flatness
near the river's mouth.
My eyes pointed—compass-spun and wanting
to gulp up that space—
pacing
the lines of perspective that drew me there
while old men cast lures off bamboo sticks,
stone-quiet if something should tug.

One was packing bait and nodded as I passed.
He had started along
the gravel while I turned to watch
the Pacific

scribbling
    off a long list of waves

and when I looked again, the man
was almost gone,
                              already a speck
surfing the haze of his distance, until two minutes
took him away

and in an hour I was gone too.

FANG

I missed the storm last night.
Everyone talked about it:
the sudden crack of sound, the way
black water and
wind thrashed the city, skinning
the rooftops.
                    But I slept through it,
exhausting my pleasure in dreams.

                    It scares me—

that the brutal fuss of thunder
passed without signaling,
that an oak might shove its trunk
through a third-storey hayloft

while I ticked undisturbed toward sunrise.

It's now I wrestle with feelings
of what I've missed, where I've not been.
It scares me how we fool ourselves, the way
anywhere becomes here.
At twenty-five, I'm afraid it'll get
elbowed away—the shock that sank,
the mutinous oath that jabbed and stuck
                    its tool of bone into youth.

I don't want to coast or lilt.

I'm afraid of the lightning-quick judgment of heaven.

There must be some chore to do, some

task to measure the progress.
Rise at six, head out and check the traps;
just to see if anything living
            has been caught in the dark.

I'm tired of the death that lies in wait, that
keeps us so close to the shoreline, tyrannized
by any uncharted reach.

I am learning to stare it in the eye
and walk over to that end,
slowly and deliberately off the edge of the world.

OMPHALOS

"Nearby was found in 1867 by Edward George Lee an astrolabe bearing the date 1603. This instrument used for determining latitude is believed to have been lost by Champlain about 7th June, 1613, on his exploratory expedition up the Ottawa River." —from a commemorative plaque located near Cobden, Ontario

From a year torn away like a page
                                        from a book,
I am curled in the car's tight womb,
driving directly through the land I know,
that Ontario far away, of
youth; rough, defiant, cragged as pine-bark,
restless as a splay of maple tattered
like rags that snap at the sky.

        This mind, this pivot—this endless
drifting that clocks my time and place
is steered by shadows, long stripes
that strap the greying blacktop, flicking across
windshields in wild projector-light.
Evening's come.
I feel that half
an hour will bring me home, spurred
on by falling dusk
and the sight of each familiar turn.

My mossy heart is breathless and almost bursting.

                                                I feel
like that boy, Edward Lee, who gave
no notice to where he was—saw
this reckless farmland imprisoned
by a grid of trees—

and lifting what
he thinks is a stone unearthed
from a fisted furrow,

finds what someone else has lost,

and not knowing what it is, or what he'll say
when he gets there,
must rush across naked fields
to tell someone anyway—

RETURN

Along a flank of the field, he lies down,
resting his skull on a headboard
of stone. His cheek is almost flush

to the gravel rolling past, dusted
by a hatching of summer mosquitoes.
Cowshit like raisins dot the dirt's surface.

He remembers now—two pigs, shot and
hoisted by hind trotters, slit from stomach
to snout, bowels globbed on the sunlit lawn.

The roomy acres stick in his head.
How he tried traversing the garden
in spring, but his boots would clump

in mud till they'd jerk and stay planted.
Or blind with sawdust, he'd thunder through
the lofts of collapsing barns, senseless

and half-afraid, threats of lockjaw gone
unheeded on afternoons so sickly hot
they lingered in the mouth like curdled milk.

When he closes his eyes, he will
picture it all and cross the dark
borders of memory. A primary survey

that was scratched into a map, he wonders
if nothing's happened since, and shudders
to think it. He'd give anything for a road

straight out of himself.

NOTES TO THE POEMS

"Soundings"

Don Antonio Pigafetta, a Venetian nobleman, was a member of Ferdinand Magellan's expedition which became the first European ocean-voyage to circumnavigate the world. After the disappointment of each false passage through South America, and a barely thwarted mutiny, Magellan successfully sailed through the straits which now bear his name, and into the Pacific. The most reliable sources of the age led them to believe that Asia would then be only a few day's sail further. Instead they endured a three-month journey, surrounded by the same flat horizon, through an ocean whose size was greatly underestimated before landfalls in Guam and the Phillipines. Euphoric and jubilant, Magellan began a fanatic conversion of the natives to Catholicism on the island of Cebu. Believing himself responsible for this new Christian island, he launched a reckless attack against the neighbouring hostile island of Mactan. Negligent of any precaution (and completely unnecessary), it proved also disastrous, resulting in Magellan's own death. Only one ship of the original five-ship armada, the *Victoria*, returned to Spain via the Indian Ocean and west-African coast. According to William Manchester, in his book, *A World Lit Only By Fire*, this voyage was the "clarifying event" of a cumulative historical process which shattered the geocentric assumptions of the medieval mind and irrevocably ushered in the Renaissance. "Europe was no longer the world, and the world was no longer the center of the universe."

The evolutionary theory, independently formulated by Charles Darwin and Alfred Russel Wallace, is generally considered to be the second great scientific revolution, refuting humanity's belief of itself as being separate from nature. When Darwin was 22 years old, he took the post of naturalist aboard the H.M.S. *Beagle*, a ten-gun brig captained by Robert FitzRoy, whose own duties included carrying out a chain of chronological reckonings around the world. Though Darwin did not form his famous theory for a number of years afterward (*On the Origin of Species by means of Natural Selection* was finally published in 1859), he later claimed that his experiences on the *Beagle* voyage (1831-36), and in particular, his contact with the diversity of life on the Galapagos Islands, led to his first doubts about the stability of species. These doubts can be already detected in his diaries of the voyage.

Chelonia mydas, the green turtle, travels 2000 miles from Brazil to Ascension Island—a tiny, volcanic island in the centre of the Atlantic Ocean—to breed, despite the fact that adequate breeding grounds are available nearby. This unnecessary journey is a puzzling anomaly in evolutionary theory.

Ikime-jinja is a small Shinto shrine located near Miyazaki City in southeastern Kyushu, Japan.

ACKNOWLEDGEMENTS

Earlier versions of some of these poems have appeared in *The Antigonish Review*, *The Fiddlehead*, *Missing Jacket*, *TickleAce*, *Vintage 95* and *Vintage 97-98* (Quarry Press), *Written in the Skin* (Insomniac Press), and *Yield*. "Axis Mundi" first appeared in *Compounds with Mixed Ligand Systems as Precursors for Thermal Synthesis of III-V Extended Solids: Halo-Pnictido, Alkyl-Pnictido, and Siloxo-Pnictido Complexes of Gallium and Indium* (Ottawa-Carleton Chemistry Institute; Department of Chemistry, University of Ottawa) by Sean Barry.

My thanks to my brother Tim, my sisters Colleen and Sharon, and their families. Also thanks to my many friends (and Sunday nights) who enriched the writing of these poems, not necessarily always in a literary way. Each of you crown a pedestal of my gratitude.

I would also like to thank the following people for their direct and generous contribution to the progress of this manuscript: Steven Heighton and Chris Swail (for their fine-tooth combs), James and Kelly Torck (for their technology), Tim Bowling, Chris Levenson, Jeff Hardill, and Jennifer Strickland of Carleton University Press.

To Ken Babstock, far more than thanks. Without his talent, terror, and unfailing friendship, I would have come nowhere in this craft. He took the other oar.

And I thank my lucky stars for Dorothy Jeffreys—for her companionship, restlessness, intelligence and love.

ALSO AVAILABLE IN THE HARBINGER POETRY SERIES

Holly Kritsch, *Something I'm Supposed to Remember*
"Holly Kritsch is an immediately attractive poet, gifted with the stern voice of raw confession. Telling of harrowing blasphemies against childhood, telling of violation and irrepressible love, her poetry matters." — *George Elliott Clarke*

Ronna Bloom, *Fear of the Ride*
"Few poets write of grief and love with such a simple elegance and an impressive depth. Ronna Bloom writes clear and hard about what hurts, and gives us hope." — *Susan Musgrave*

Anne Le Dressay, *Sleep is a Country*
"Have you heard rocks keening? Anne Le Dressay helps us recognize the sound. Austere as ancient standing stones, her poems are perfectly shaped, perfectly positioned to reflect the wordless light." — *Mary A. Wright*

Mark Sinnett, *The Landing*
1998 winner of the League of Canadian Poets' Gerald Lampert Award for the best first book of poetry in the previous year.
"These poems [are] blessedly unphoney and clearvoiced ... quite often piercingly unexpected, moving, right."
— *Don Coles*

Craig Poile's collection, *First Crack*
"By turns playful, ironic, elegaic, Craig Poile in this carefully observed first collection runs the gamut of human experience. It treats both historical and contemporary subjects in a sensitive, eccentric manner, capturing those moments where history and the present, art and the life of the observer, collide."
— *The Judges of the Gerald Lampert Memorial Award, 1999*

Michelle Desbarats, *Last Child to Come Inside*
"This is poetry full of quick and acutely angled insight, moving with great sureness to glimpse the raven's wing inside the ordinary." — *Don McKay*

Eleonore Schönmaier, *Treading Fast Rivers*
"In this collection rediscovered gifts abound. Schönmaier's clear, strong writing, steeped in water and sky, gull bone and moonlight, maps for us the geography of fathers, of illness and of love. These poems have a keen sense of direction and have found more than one way of recognizing truth." — *Susan Goyette*